# TABLE OF CONTENTS

# Caffè SHAKERATO

Ingredients

1 espresso
&
ice cubes

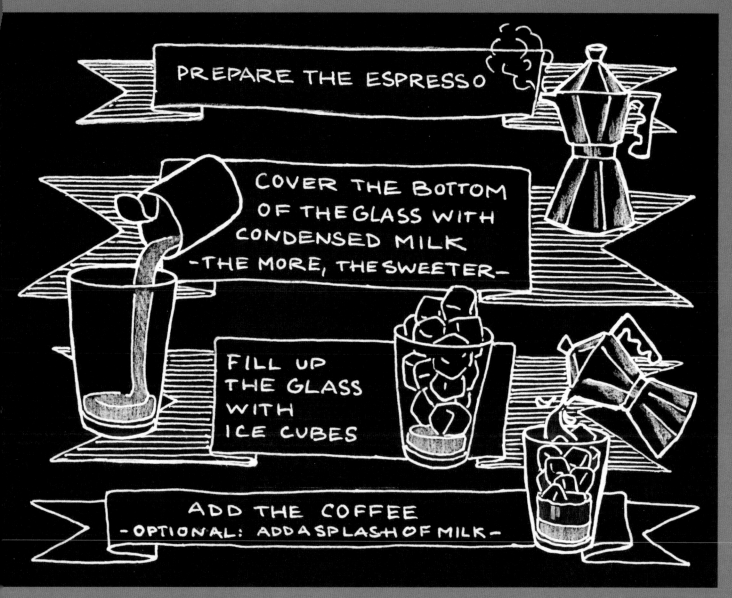

boiled water =

Herb Tea

# Ingredients for this awesome cocktail:

- a glass of tomato juice
- a squeeze of lemon juice
- worcester sauce, to taste
- ground pepper, to taste
- tabasco sauce, to taste
- celery stick for garnish
- lemon wedge for garnish

# Virgin Mary

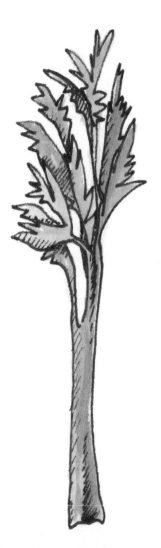

RUB RIMS OF 6 GLASSES WITH A WEDGE OF LIME

SPIN RIM OF EACH GLASS IN A SAUCER WITH SALT

SO THE RIMS ARE SALT COATED

3 1/2 CUP

1/2 CUP

CUBED & CHILLED

TEQUILA

# Cucumber-Mint MARGARITA

1/3 CUP TEQUILA

1/4 CUP LIME JUICE

1/2 CUP DICED CUCUMBER

1/4 CUP CHOPPED MINT

shaken, not stirred

6 ICE CUBES

SALT & PEPPER & CUMIN POWDER

# french onion soup

pepper

BUTTER

40 grams

600 grams

onions

peeled & sliced

• In a pan, melt the butter and then softly sauté the onions • Leave on very low heat for about 15 minutes • Then on medium heat, give it another 10 minutes, stirring regularly, until the onions have turned golden brown • Add stock and bay leaves • Let simmer for about 30 minutes • Season with a little pepper and discard bay leaves

1 liter
Beef Stock

2
Bay leaves

120 grams
Swiss Gruyère cheese

Toast 8 baguette slices

Preheat oven grill

Ladle soup into 4 oven-proof soup bowls

Put toast on top of soups & sprinkle with cheese

Put bowls under the grill until cheese bubbles...

...and is slightly browned

Serve immediately

secret:
you can add a splash of Cognac

# Celeriac Soup

* a splash of olive oil
* 1 celeriac, peeled and diced
* 1 liter vegetable stock
* 2 onions, peeled and diced
* 4 garlic cloves, peeled and chopped
* a handful of parsley, finely chopped

Sauté the onion and celeriac in some olive oil

add garlic

Add Stock

Let simmer for about 20 minutes

on low heat

leave a little bit of parsley for garnish

add parsley

Spoon the soup into bowls

use a hand-held blender to make a smooth soup

Garnish with parsley and a few drops of olive oil

fry garlic, shallots and chilli pepper
in some olive oil

add the peas and saffron

add 1 liter of boiling water
and the stock

bring to boil and let simmer
for 10 minutes

add mint leaves and whizz
with (hand held) blender

400 GRAMS of GREEN PEAS
2 SHALLOTS, chopped
24 THREADS of SAFFRON
2 TABLETS of HERB STOCK
½ CHILLI PEPPER
2 CLOVES of GARLIC } chopped
10 FRESH MINT LEAVES

PINK SALAD

1 BEETROOT (PRE-COOKED)

1 TABLESPOON OF GREEK YOGURT OR QUARK

A SQUEEZE OF LEMON JUICE

SALT

PEPPER

A HANDFUL OF ROASTED SESAME SEEDS

1 TEASPOON OF MAYO

A FEW LEAVES OF MINT CHOPPED

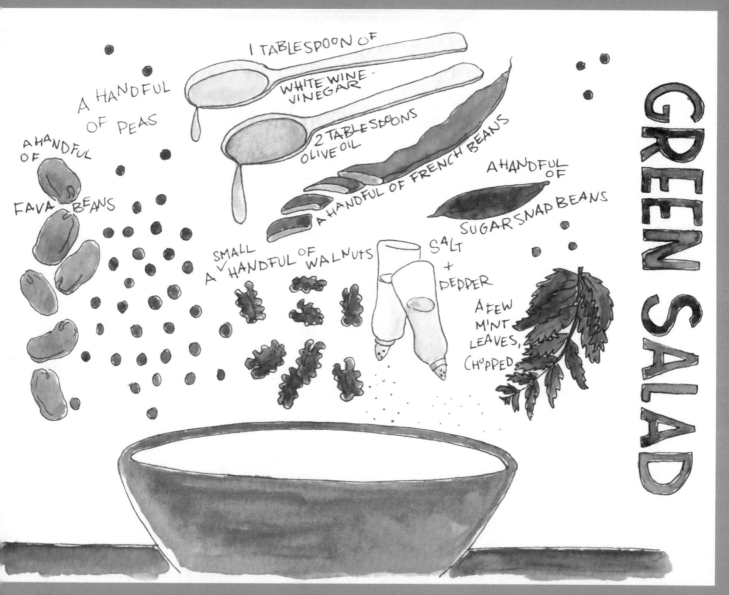

# Kale!

## Chips

## Green Smoothie

2 cups Kale
1/2 cup water
1 orange
1/2 banana
1" ginger root
2 tsp. lime juice

S

22

# Stir-Fry

100 grams kale
2 Tbsp. olive oil
pinch of salt

Toss all ingredients
together in a bowl.
Spread them on
2 large oven trays
with baking paper.
Bake in oven
on 200 C/395 F
for 12-15 minutes.
Cools in 30 secs.

3 Tbsp. peanut oil
200 grams Kale
2 garlic cloves
1 red chilli
2 Tbsp. fish sauce

Heat oil on high heat.
Add Kale, garlic, chilli.
Stir-fry on high heat for
4-5 minutes.  Remove
from heat.  Add fish
sauce.  Serve with rice.

# PEPPERS IN OIL

- GET RID OF THE PEPPERS' STEMS AND SEEDS.
- CUT PEPPERS INTO STRIPS.
- CUT THE GARLIC CLOVES IN HALF.
- BRING 600 ML OF WATER AND THE VINEGAR TO THE BOIL.
- ADD PEPPERS AND A PINCH OF SALT.
- BOIL THIS FOR 8 MINUTES. DRAIN.
- MIX IN SOME PEPPER+SALT, PUT IT ALL IN POTS, AND FILL UP WITH OLIVE OIL.
- STORE IN THE FRIDGE (MAX. 2 WEEKS).

1 RED PEPPER

1 GREEN PEPPER

1 YELLOW PEPPER

5 CLOVES OF GARLIC

OLIVE OIL

150 ML RED WINE VINEGAR

SALT & PEPPER

- 120 grams Green Papaya - Grated
- 1 tablespoon Dried Shrimps
- 1 tablespoon Birds eyes chillies
- 1 cup Long beans
  - cut into 1-inch pieces
- 1-2 Garlic Cloves
- 1 tablespoon Palm Sugar
- 4 table spoons Lime Juice
- 8 Cherry tomatoes
  - cut in halves
- 4 table spoons Fish Sauce
- 2 tablespoons Roasted Peanuts

Pound garlic and chillies into a paste using mortar and pestle. Add long beans and crush them a bit with the pestle. Pound together adding the green papaya and stir with a spoon between poundings, until well blended. Add dried shrimps, tomatoes, palm sugar, fish sauce and lime juice, gently pound and stir until blended.

Taste and add more lime juice, palm sugar or chillies if needed.

Before serving, sprinkle with roasted peanuts.

# Som tam
## (Green Papaya Salad)

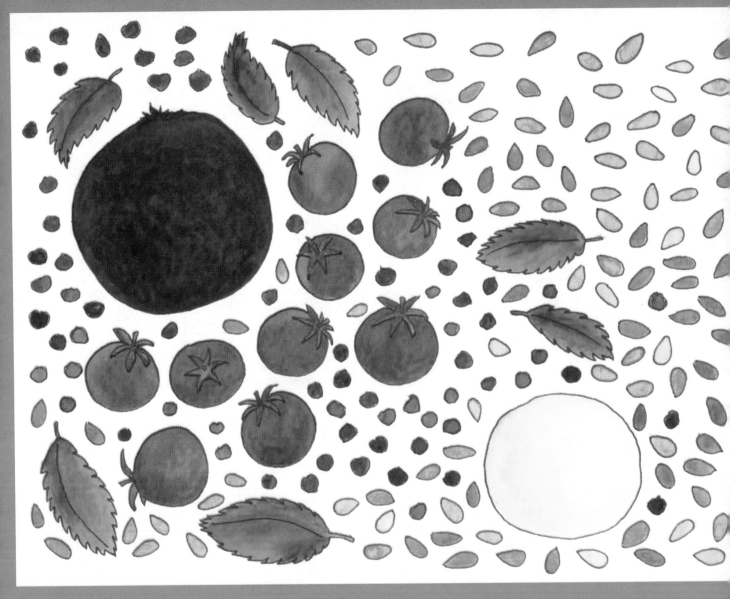

# Warm oven-Salad

## Ingredients

- 1 piece of beetroot (pre-cooked)
- 10 cherry tomatoes
- A handful of fresh mint leaves
- Mozzarella cheese
- 2 table spoons of capers
- 2 table spoons of roasted pine nuts
- olive oil
- Salt and pepper

— serves two —

1. pre-heat oven 180°C
2. pierce tomatoes, so they won't 'pop' in the oven
3. Cut the beetroot into bite-size pieces
4. put tomatoes in an oven dish or plate, and the beetroot in another.
5. Sprinkle olive oil, salt and pepper over them, and place both dishes in the oven for about 15 minutes.
6. Let cool off a bit.
7. Arrange on a large plate: beets first, then the tomatoes.
8. Tear the cheese into pieces, place on top
9. Tear mint leaves, and sprinkle these over the plate, along with the capers and pine nuts.

5 potatoes, washed-leave skins on
1 bunch of chives
4 tablespoons of Greek yoghurt
2 tablespoons of prepared horseradish
1 tablespoon of mayonaise
   Salt & pepper

1 Boil the potatoes, drain,
   when cooled, cut them into wedges
2 Finely chop the chives
3 Mix yoghurt, mayo and horseradish,
   add salt and pepper, to your taste
4 Combine with the potatoes and chives

1 can

chick
peas

(about
250 grams)

salt
.1 tsp.

ginger
.1 tablespoon.
sirup

olive oil
.2 tablespoons.

(dried chili flakes
.1 teaspoon.

tahini
(sesame paste)
.2 tablespoons.

# Healthy Hummus

.4 tablespoons.
lemon juice

.2 teaspoons.
cumin powder

Use a food processor to combine all ingredients until smooth

insalata

# di arance

sicilian style

1 orange
1 spoon of chili flakes
olive oil
a pinch (or two) of salt

*peel and cut the orange into
bite size pieces, put them
on a plate.
*sprinkle them with salt and
peperoncini.

* Generously dress your
salad with olive oil.

1 CAN/JAR
Chick Peas

8 tomatoes
peeled and sliced

2 red peppers
sliced into strips

1 onion → chopped

4 garlic cloves

1 tsp. paprika

3 (fresh) bay leaves

small dot of saffron threads

how to peel?

boil water

cut undeep crosses into the tomato skins

top + bottom

put in a bowl for 5-10 minutes

drain & peel skins off

2 tsp. rosemary finely chopped

100 ml

vegetable stock

## SOAK
saffron threads in a few spoons boiling water

## SAUTÉ
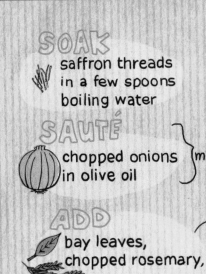
chopped onions in olive oil — **15 minutes**

## ADD
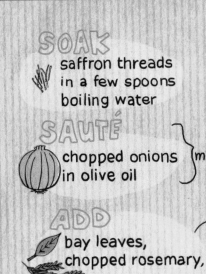
bay leaves, chopped rosemary, chopped garlic, sliced peppers — **another 10 minutes**

## ADD
chopped tomatoes + paprika — **10 more minutes**

## ADD
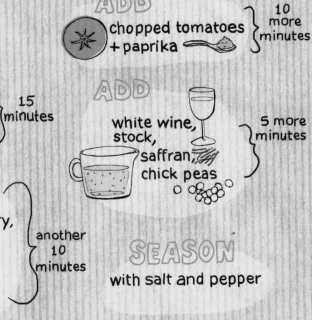
white wine, stock, saffran, chick peas — **5 more minutes**

## SEASON
with salt and pepper

6 tablespoons olive oil

150 ml white wine

# VEGETABLE STEW

nice with rice

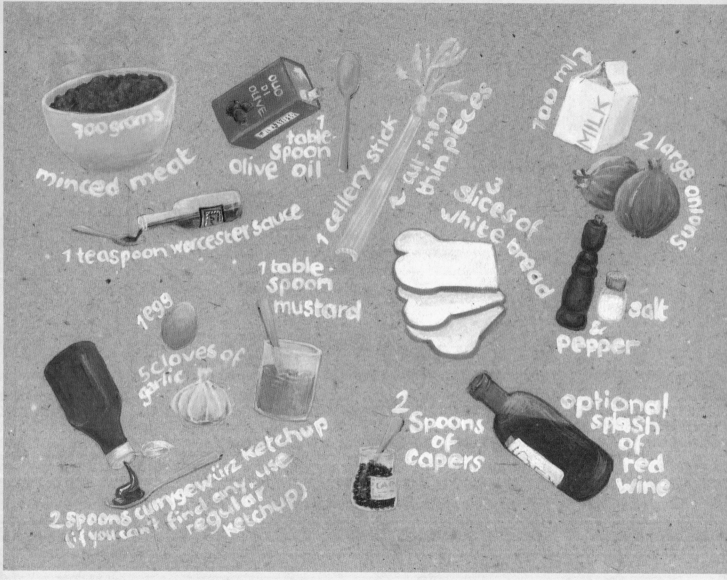

700 grams minced meat

1 tablespoon olive oil

1 celery stick

cut into thin pieces

3 slices of white bread

700 ml milk

2 large onions

1 teaspoon worcester sauce

1 tablespoon mustard

salt & pepper

1 egg

5 cloves of garlic

2 spoons currygewürz ketchup (if you can't find any, use regular ketchup)

2 spoons of capers

optional splash of red wine

38

# meatloaf

-Preheat the oven to 200°C.

-Lightly fry the finely chopped onion, garlic and cellery in a bit of olive oil.

-Cut the crusts of the bread and let the bread soak in the milk for 5 minutes. After this, take the bread out and squeeze excessive milk out.

-Put the minced meat, sauce, ketchup, egg, capers, onion/garlic/cellery, bread, pepper and salt and knead everything together.

-Line a cake tin with aluminumfoil. On top of the foil-lining, line with baking paper.

-Put the mix into the tin, press softly so the corners are filled, too. Around the edges, create a 'drainage channel' around the loaf, by pressing the meat down around the edges. This way any bubbling fat can get away without making a burned mess in your oven.

-Cover the filled tin with foil and put in the preheated oven for 50 minutes.

-Take of the foil cover and give it another ten minutes.

-Take your meatloaf out of the oven, let it cool of and take out of the tin.

-Cut into thick slices and serve with horse radish sauce.

plus:

For this
simple horse radish sauce
mix these ingredients:

-6 tablespoons of sour cream
-2 tablespoons of horse radish
-pepper
-salt
(if you have any, you can add
some finely chopped chives)

Ingredients for 4 portions:
400 grams spaghetti
250 grams pancetta
2 small shallots
black pepper
2 eggs
150 grams parmesan cheese
olive oil

* Cut the shallots into small pieces and cut the pancetta in ribbons.
* Put a pan of water on the stove for the spaghetti. Bring to boil.
* Heat a pan and bake the pancetta softly.
* In the meantime, add the spaghetti to the boiling water.
* As soon as the pancetta is hot, add the shallots and fry until soft. Then take off the stove.
* Strain of the al dente pasta, but keep a little bit of the water.
* Put the pancetta and shallots back on the fire and add the spaghetti. Bake this all for a minute.
* Add a bit of the pasta water (about half a cup)
* Grind some black pepper over it, to your taste.
* Take the pan off the fire and after that: break the two eggs and stir well but carefully.
* Serve with some olive oil and grated parmesan.

spaghetti
carbonara

# Quick Pasta

Fusili, or any kind of pasta you like

cook it

1 onion

chop it up

Sauté!

# Dinner

a squeeze (or more) of lemon juice

drain the pasta

and add

add sardines

stir gently

# home made SODA BREAD

500 grams flour

1 teaspoon baking soda

1 teaspoon salt

POUR INTO A BAKING TRAY

MIX ALL INGREDIENTS

1/2 liter butter milk

BAKE FOR 40 MINUTES

IN A PREHEATED OVEN 230°C 446 F

# CHOC·O-spread

juice of 1 orange

blend ingredients into a smooth paste.
* too runny?
↳ add more cocoa powder
* too dry?
↳ add more juice

20 dried dates
remove stones & crowns

80 grams of unsweetened cocoa powder.

Spoon into a clean jar. cover and keep refrigerated

**Option:** spoon a handful of cocoa nibs through the mixture.

## Serving Suggestions:

| spread on a slice of bread or toast | use as icing on cake | make truffles: roll small balls through cocoa powder | Serve in small glasses as a dessert |
| --- | --- | --- | --- |
|  |  |  |  |

# Raw & Sugar-less

1 Tbsp. zest

3 Tbsp. Orange juice

50 grams cocoa nibs

3 Tbsp. Grated coconut
+ 2 extra for later

put on plate and set aside

8 dried dates
take stones out and chop them

GUILT-FREE!

these guys make the bon-bons sweet like honey!

48

# Bon Bons

① crush cocoa nibs, then add dates, juice, and zest

② mix coconut in.

③ use your hands to make little balls

yes, your hands will become sticky, but hey, you wanted to coo?, right?

④ roll balls through coconut on a plate

⑤ keep refrigerated or serve right away

# Super Simple coconut

leave the egg yolks out!

2 EGG WHITES

SUGAR

110 grams SUGAR

GRATED COCONUT

180 grams GRATED COCONUT

LEMON ZEST
(of ½ a lemon)

you can also use lime

# balls

mix well

make small balls and
place them on a baking tray*

* lined with baking sheet

180 °C / 350 °F

± 10 minutes until golden brown

I ♥ CHOCOLATE

1 cup of cornflakes

150 grams of Chocolate

Pour the cornflakes into the bowl with melted chocolate.
Stir gently.
until all is well blended.

Break the chocolate into pieces and place them in a bowl!

microwave

let the chocolate melt, 30 seconds a time, then stir, put it back into the microwave and do this again and again until the chocolate has melted

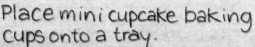

Place mini cupcake baking cups onto a tray.

Spoon small mounds of the chocolate-cornflakes-mix ......

Your patience will be rewarded with these

# Corn flakes - Chocolate treats

Place the tray into the fridge for ½ hour

Isn't that the most fun part of cooking?

this is the moment to taste, spill and lick your fingers a lot!
Because later on you'll need some patience before eating the treats.

....into the cups

I ♥ CHOCOLATE

pour yogurt into clean tea towell on top of a bowl. Use a rubber band

Cover with plastic foil. Leave for ± 5 hours

to hold in place

Serves 2

# Autumn Dessert

discard fluid + stones of the dates

add cinnamon

whizz it

Slice plums & grill them

ø ± 1cm

Tile plumb slices onto plate, and

Serve with the strained cinnamon yogurt

- 2 plums
- 3 dried dates
- 400 grams Bulgarian yogurt
- 2 tablespoons of cinnamon

# Cheesecake

 150 grams tea biscuits

 2 eggs
2 egg yolks

 150 grams butter

 550 grams cream cheese

 pinch of salt

 150 grams sugar

 2 tsp. cinnamon

Preheat oven

190°C
375 °F

Mix

cookies

melted butter

pinch of salt

Line side of a springform cake tin with baking paper

23 Ø cm

cover bottom with cookie mixture

Mix

Cream cheese

eggs & yolks

sugar

optional:

add 1 tbsp lemon juice and zest

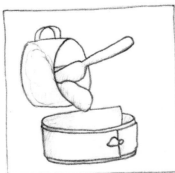

Bake for 25 minutes

Let cool of

optional: spread with jam and/or fresh fruit

Plum jam

enjoy!

PREP WORK:

1 WASH * 2 ORANGES PUT IN PAN OF BOILING WATER, PUT THE LID ON, BOIL ON VERY LOW HEAT FOR 1,5 HOUR

GET RID OF WATER MASH ORANGES SKIN'N'ALL!

3 MASH 'EM!

4 ADD * 20 DRIED DATES STONES REMOVED!

COMBINE WITH EGGS + ZEST OF * 1 LEMON

AND MIX

2 BREAK * 6 EGGS

5 AND MIX

going

**6** STIR IN:
* ½ TEASPOON BICARB
* 250 GRAMS ALMOND FLOUR
* 1 TEASPOON BAKING POWDER

**7** POUR INTO
* BUTTERED CAKE TIN

→ THEN COVER WITH TIN FOIL

**8** BAKE IN OVEN PREHEATED!
180°C   350°F

FOR 30 MINUTES

→ AND BAKE

FOR ANOTHER 15 MINUTES

**9** LET COOL ON A RACK AND SERVE WITH
* SHAVED ALMONDS SPRINKLED ON TOP.

# NUTS for this cake!

# Christmas tree Cookies

preheat oven to 180 °C

220 grams softened butter
100 grams white bastard sugar
1 egg yolk
250 grams flour
2 teaspoons cinnamon
pinch of salt

For the icing:
1 egg white, lightly beaten,
250 grams icing sugar,
cake decoration

baking parchment
plastic wrap
cookie cutters
rolling pin
coloured ribbons
large straw

**1** mix butter and sugar
until creamy
then add the egg yolk and mix

**2** sift flour, salt and
cinnamon into mixture
and stir until combined

**3** shape dough into 2 balls,
wrap them in plastic wrap
and chill them in the
refrigerator for about 30 minutes

**4** roll out the dough

stamp out cookies and stamp out rounds
in the top of each shape, using a straw

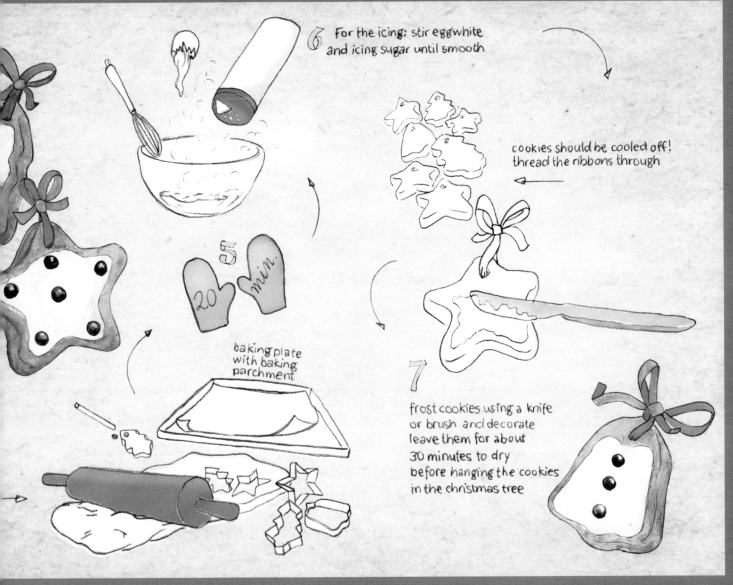

6 For the icing: stir eggwhite and icing sugar until smooth

cookies should be cooled off! thread the ribbons through

baking plate with baking parchment

7

frost cookies using a knife or brush and decorate leave them for about 30 minutes to dry before hanging the cookies in the christmas tree

20 & min.

# THEY DRAW & COOK™

**FOOD INK: 30 Illustrated Recipes**
**by Koosje Koene**

Conceived, designed and produced
by Studio SSS and Koosje Koene

## STUDIO SSS, LLC

Nate Padavick & Salli Swindell
studiosss.tumblr.com

## KOOSJE KOENE

koosjekoene.nl
sketchbookskool.com

## Conversions

### Common Measurement Equivalents

3 TS = 1 TBS = 1/2 FL OZ
2 TS = 1 FL OZ
4 TS = 2 FL OZ = 1/4 C
8 TBS = 4 FL OZ = 1/2 C
16 TBS = 8 FL OZ = 1 C
16 FL OZ = 2 C = 1 PT
32 FL OZ = 4 C = 2 PT = 1 QT
128 FL OZ = 16 C = 8 PT = 4 QT = 1 G

### Volume

| | |
|---|---|
| 1 TS | 5 ML |
| 1 TBS | 15 ML |
| 1/4 C | 59 ML |
| 1 C | 236 ML |
| 1 PT | 472 ML |
| 1 QT | 944 ML |
| 1 G | 3.8 L |

### Length

| | |
|---|---|
| 1 IN | 2.54 CM |
| 4 IN | 10 CM |
| 6 IN | 5 CM |
| 8 IN | 20 CM |
| 9 IN | 23 CM |
| 10 IN | 25 CM |
| 12 IN | 30 CM |
| 13 IN | 33 CM |

### Weight/Mass

| | |
|---|---|
| 1/4 OZ | 7 G |
| 1/3 OZ | 10 G |
| 1/2 OZ | 14 G |
| 1 OZ | 28 G |
| 2 OZ | 57 G |
| 3 OZ | 85 G |
| 4 OZ | 113 G |
| 5 OZ | 142 G |
| 6 OZ | 170 G |
| 7 OZ | 198 G |
| 8 OZ | 227 G |
| 9 OZ | 255 G |
| 10 OZ | 284 G |
| 11 OZ | 312 G |
| 12 OZ | 340 G |
| 13 OZ | 369 G |
| 14 OZ | 397 G |
| 15 OZ | 425 G |
| 16 OZ | 454 G |

### Oven Temperatures

| | |
|---|---|
| 300°F | 150°C |
| 325°F | 165°C |
| 350°F | 180°C |
| 375°F | 190°C |
| 400°F | 200°C |
| 425°F | 220°C |
| 450°F | 230°C |
| 475°F | 245°C |

### Helpful Formulas

Tablespoons x 14.79 = Milliliters
Cups x 0.236 = Liters
Ounces x 28.35 = Grams
Degrees F − 32 x 5 ÷ 9 = Degrees C
Inches x 2.54 = Centimeters

Made in the USA
Lexington, KY
26 August 2015